FREE AGENCY AND THE WILL

ROBERT LEWIS DABNEY

Title	Free Agency and the Will
Creator	Robert Lewis Dabney
Rights	Public Domain
Published By Parables	
	November, 2016

All Rights Reserved. No part of this book may be reproduced or utilized in any form or by any means, electronic or mechanical, including photocopying, recording, or by any information storage and retrieval system, without permission in writing from the author.

Unless otherwise specified Scripture quotations are taken from the authorized version of the King James Bible.

ISBN 978-1-945698-07-1
Printed in the United States of America

Readers should be aware that Internet Web sites offered as citations and/or sources for further information may have been changed or disappeared between the time this was written and when it is read.

Illustration provided by www.unsplash.com

FREE AGENCY
AND THE WILL

ROBERT LEWIS DABNEY

PUBLISHED by PARABLES
Earthly Stories with a Heavenly Meaning

1.
MAN A FREE AGENT, DENIED BY TWO PARTIES

UT is man a free agent? Many have denied it. These may be ranked under two classes, Theological Fatalists and Sensualistic Necessitarians. The former argue from the doctrine of God's foreknowledge and providence; the latter from the certainty, or, as it has unluckily been termed, necessity of the Will. Say the one party; God has foreknown and foreordained all that is done by rational man, as well as by irrational elements, and His almighty providence infallibly effectuates it all. Therefore, man's will is only seemingly free; he must be a machine; compelled by God (for if God had no efficacious means to compel, He could not certainly have foreknown) to do what God purposed from eternity: and, therefore, man never had any real choice; he is the slave of this divine fate. Say the other party, headed by Hobbes: man's volitions are all effects: following with a physical necessity upon the movement of the preponderant desires. But what are his desires? The soul intrinsically is passive; the attributes are nothing but certain susceptibilities of being affected in certain ways, by impressions from without. There is nothing, no thought, no feeling in the mind, except what sensation produced there; indeed all inward states are but modified sensations. Hence, desire is but the reflex of the perception of a desirable object; resentment but the Reformed-action from impact. Man's emotions, then, are the physical results of outward impressions, and his volitions the necessary effects of his emotions. Man's whole volitions, therefore, are causatively determined from without. While he supposes himself free, he is the slave of circumstances: of fate, if those circumstances arise by chance.

Replies to Them

Now, in answer to all this, it would be enough to say, that our consciousness contradicts it. There can be no higher evidence than that of consciousness. Every man feels conscious that wherever he has power to do what he wills, he acts freely. And the validity of this uniform, immediate testimony of consciousness, as

Cousin well remarks, on this subject, must, in a sense, supersede all other evidence of our free-agency; because all possible premises of such. arguments must depend on the testimony of consciousness. But still it is correct to argue, that man must be a free agent; because this is inevitably involved in his responsibility. Conscience tells us we are responsible for our moral acts. Reason pronounces, intuitively, that responsibility would be absurd were we not free agents. It may be well added, that when you approach revealed theology, you find the Scriptures, (which so frequently assert God's decree and providence,) assert and imply, with equal frequency, man's free-agency. The king of Babylon (Isaiah 14) fulfills God's purpose in capturing the sinful Jews; but he also fulfills the purpose of his own heart. But we can do more than rebut the

Fatalist's views by the testimony of our consciousness; we can expose their sophistry. God's mode of effectuating His purposes as to the acts of free agents, is not by compelling their acts or wills, contrary to their preferences and dispositions; either secretly or openly; but by operating through their dispositions. And as to the latter argument, from the certainty of the will; we repudiate the whole philosophy of sensationalism, from which it arises. True, volitions are effects; but not effects of the objects upon which they go forth. The perception of these is but the occasion of their rise, not the cause. When desire attaches itself upon any external object, terminating in volition, the whole activity and power are in the mind, not in the object. The true immediate cause of volition is the mind's own previous view and feeling; and, this, again is the result of the minds' spontaneity, as guided by its own prevalent attributes and habitudes.

2.
FREEDOM AND NECESSITY DEFINED. SEMI-PELAGIANISM AND CALVINISTS

What constitutes man a free agent? Say one party: the self-determining power of the will; say the other: the self-determining power of the soul. The one asserts that our acts of volition are uncaused phenomena, that the will remains in *equilibrio*, after all the preliminary conditions of judgment in the understanding, and emotion of the native dispositions are fulfilled, and that the act of choice is self-determined by the will, and not by the preliminary states of soul tending thereto; so that volitions are in every case, more or less contingent. The other party repudiates, indeed, the old sensational creed, of a physical tie between the external objects which are the occasions of our judgments and feelings; and attributes all action of will to the soul's own spontaneity as its efficient source. But it asserts that this spontaneity, like all other forces in the universe, acts according to law; that this law is the connection between the soul's own states and its own choices, the former being as much of its own spontaneity as the latter; that therefore volitions are uncaused, but always follow the actual state of judgment and feeling, (single or complex) at the time being; and that this connection is not contingent, but efficient and certain. And this certainty is all that they mean by moral necessity.

3.
WILL DETERMINED BY SUBJECTIVE MOTIVE. ARGUMENTS

The latter is evidently the true doctrine: because,

(a) Our consciousness says so. Everyman feels that when he acts, as a thinking being, he has a motive for acting so; and that if he had not had, he would not have done it. The man is conscious that he determines himself, else, he would not be free; but he is equally conscious that it is himself judging and desiring, which determines himself choosing:

(b) Otherwise there would be no such thing as a recognition of character, or permanent principles. For there would be no efficient influence of the man's own principles over his actions; (and it is by his actions alone we would know his principles;) and his principles might be of a given character, and his actions summum bonum of a different, or of no character.

(c) Consequently there would be no certain result from human influence over man's character and actions, in education and moral government. We might educate the principles, and still fail to educate the actions and habits. The fact which we all experience every day would be impossible, that we can cause our fellow-men to put forth certain volitions, that we can often do it with a foreseen certainty, and still we feel that those acts are free and responsible.

(d) Otherwise man might be neither a reasonable nor a moral being. Not reasonable, because his acts might be wholly uncontrolled at last by his whole understanding; not moral, because the merit of an act depends on its motive, and his acts would be motiveless. The self-determined volition has its freedom essentially in this, according to its advocates; that it is caused by no motive. Hence, no acts are free and virtuous, except those which a man does without having any reason for them. Is this good sense? Does not the virtuousness of a man's acts depend upon the kind of reason which moved to them?

(e) In the choice of one's *summum bonum*, the will is certainly not contingent. Can a rational being choose his own misery, apprehended as such, and eschew his own happiness, for their own sakes? Yet that choice is free; and if certainty is compatible with free-agency in this the most important case, why not in any other?

(f) God, angels, saints in glory, and the human nature of Jesus Christ, must be certainly determined to right volitions by the holiness of their own natures, and in all but the first case by the indwelling grace and the determinate purpose of God. So, on the other hand, lost souls, and those who on earth have sinned away their day of grace, must be certainly determined to evil, by their own decisive evil natures and habits: yet their choice is free in both cases.

(g) If the will were contingent, there could be no *scientia media*, and we should be compelled to the low and profane ground of the Socinian; that God does not certainly foreknow all things and in the nature of things, cannot. For the definition of *scientia media* is, that it is that contingent knowledge of what free agents will do in certain foreseen circumstances, arising out of God's infinite insight into their dispositions. But if the will may decide in the teeth of that foreseen disposition, there can be no certain knowledge how it will decide. Nor is the evasion suggested by modern Arminians (vide, Mansel's Lim. of Relig. Thought) of ally force; that it is incompetent for our finite understandings to say that God cannot have this scientia media, because we cannot see how He is to have it. For the thing is not merely among the incomprehensible, but the impossible. If a thing is certainly foreseen, it must be certain to occur, or else the foreknowledge of its certain occurrence is false. But if it is certain to occur, it must be because there will be an antecedent, certainly, or efficiently connected with the event, as cause. It is, therefore, in the knowledge of this causal connection, that God would find his *scientia media*, if this branch of His knowledge were mediate. To sum up in a word, the inutility of this evasion, this Semi-Pelagian theory begins by imputing to God an inferential knowledge of man's free acts, and then, in denying the certain influence of motives takes away the only ground of inference.

(h) Last, God would have no efficient means of governing free agents; things would be perpetually emerging through their contingent acts, unforeseen by God, and across His purposes; and His government would be, like man's, one of sorry expedients to patch up His failures. Nor could He bestow any certain answer to prayer, either for our own protection against temptation and wrong choice, or the evil acts of other free agents. All the predictions of Scripture concerning events in which the free moral acts of rational agents enter as second causes, are arguments against the contingency of the will. But we see striking instances in Joseph, the Assyrians, Cyrus, and especially the Jews who rejected their Lord. From this point of view, the celebrated argument of Edwards for the certainty of the will from God's foreknowledge of creatures' free acts, is obvious. The solution of the cavils attempted against it is this position: That the principle, "No event without a cause," which is, to us, a universal and necessary first truth, is also a truth to the divine mind. When God certainly foresees an act. He foresees it as coming certainly out of its cause. Hence, I repeat, if the foresight is certain, the causation must be efficient.

4
CERTAINTY OF THE WILL PROVED BY GOD'S SOVEREIGNTY

I have indicated, both when speaking of fatalism and of the impossibility of a scientia media concerning a contingent will, the argument for the certainty of the will contained in the fact of God's sovereignty. If He is universal First Cause, then nothing is uncaused. Such is the argument; as simple as it is comprehensive. It cannot be taught that volitions are uncaused, unless you make all free agents a species of gods, independent of Jehovah's control. In other words, if His providence extends to the acts of free agents, their volitions cannot be uncaused; for providence includes control, and control implies power. The argument from God's sovereignty is, indeed, so conclusive, that the difficulty, with thinking minds, is not to admit it, but to avoid being led by it to an extreme. The difficulty rather is, to see how, in the presence of this universal absolute sovereignty, man can retain a true spontaneity. I began by defining that, while the will of man is not self-determining, his soul is. I believe that a free, rational Person does properly originate effects; that he is a true fountain of spontaneity, determining his own powers, from within, to new effects. This is a most glorious part of that image of God, in which he is created. This is free-agency! Now, how can this fact be reconciled with what we have seen of God as absolute First Cause?

(j) The demonstration may be closed by the famous Reductio ad absurdum, which Edwards has borrowed from the scholastics. If the will is not determined to choice by motives, but determines itself, then the will must determine itself thereto by an act of choice; for this is the will's only function. That is, the will must choose to choose. Now, this prior choice must be held by our opponents to be self-determined. Then it must be determined by the will's act of choice—I. e., the will must choose to choose to choose. Thus we have a ridiculous and endless regressus.

I now return to consider the objections usually advanced against our doctrine. The most formidable is that which shall be first introduced; the supposed incompatibility of God's sovereignty as universal First Cause, with man's freedom.

Yet Man under Providence is free

The reconciliation may and does transcend our comprehension, and yet be neither unreasonable nor incredible. The point where the little circle of creature volition inosculates with the immense circle of the divine will, is beyond human view. When we remember that the wisdom, power and resources of God are infinite, it is not hard to see that there may be a way by which our spontaneity is directed, omnipotently, and yet without infringement of its reality. The sufficient proof is, that we, finite creatures, can often efficaciously direct the free will of our fellows, without infringing it. Does any one say that still, in every such case, the agent, if free as to us, has power to do the opposite of what we induce him to do? True, he has physical power. But yet the causative efficacy of our means is certain; witness the fact that we were able certainly to predict our success. A perfect certainty, such as results from God's infinitely wise and powerful providence over the creature's will, is all that we mean by moral necessity. We assert no other kind of necessity over the free will. More mature reflection shows us, that so far are God's sovereignty and providence from infringing man's free-agency, they are its necessary conditions. Consider: What would the power of choice be worth to one if there were no stability in the laws of nature; or no uniformity in its powers? No natural means of effectuating volitions would have any certainty, whence choice would be impotent, and motives would cease to have any reasonable weight. Could you intelligently elect to sow, if there were no ordinance of nature insuring seed time and harvest? But now, what shall give that stability to nature? A mechanical, physical necessity? That results in naught but fatalism. The only other answer is: it must be the intelligent purpose of an almighty, personal God.

    The leading objections echoed by Arminians against the certainty of the will, is, that if man is not free from all constraint, whether of motive or co-action, it is unjust in God to hold him subject to blame, or to command to those acts against which His will is certainly determined, or to punishments for failure. We reply, practically, that men are held blamable and punishable for acts to which their wills are certainly determined, both among men and before God; and all consciences approve. This is indisputable, in the case of those who are overmastered by a malignant emotion, as in Gen. 37:4, of devils and lost souls, and of those who have sinned away their day of grace. The Arminian rejoins,(Watson, vol. 2, p. 438:) Such transgressors, notwithstanding their inability of will, are justly held responsible for all subsequent failures in duty, because they sinned away the contingency of their own wills, by their own personal, free act, after they became intelligent agents. But as man is born in this inability of will, through an arrangement with a federal head, to which he had no opportunity to dissent, it would be unjust in God to hold him responsible, unless He had restored the contingency of will to them lost in Adam, by the common sufficient grace bestowed through Christ. But the distinction is worthless: 1st, because, then, God would have been under an obligation in righteousness, to furnish a plan of redemption: but the Scriptures represent His act therein as purely gracious. 2d. Because, then, all the guilt of the subsequent sins of those who had thrown away the contingency of their own wills; would have inhered in the acts alone by which they lost it. True; that act would have been an enormously guilty one; the man would have therein committed moral suicide. But it would also be true that the man was thereafter morally dead, and the dead cannot work. 3d. The Arminian should, by parity of reason, conclude, that in any will certainly determined to holiness, the acts are not meritorious, unless that determination resulted from the being's own voluntary self-culture, and formation of good dispositions and habits. Therefore God's will, which has been from eternity certainly determined to good, does nothing meritorious! [*]

But the more analytical answer to this class of objections is: that the certainty of disobedience in the sinner's will is no excuse for him, because it proceeds from a voluntary cause—i.e., moral disposition. As the volition is only the man willing, the motive is the man feeling; it is the man's self. There is no lack of the requisite capacities, if the man would use those capacities aright. Now, a man cannot plead the existence of an obstacle as his excuse, which consists purely in his own spontaneous emission of opposition.

THAT THIS MAKES US MACHINES

Now, the objections most confidently urged, are: (a.) That our view makes man a machine, an intelligent one, indeed; but a machine in which choice follows motive by a physical tie. Ans. Man is in one sense a machine, (if you will use so inappropriate an illustration); his spontaneous force of action has its regular laws. But he is not a machine, in the essential point; the motive power is not external, but is in himself.

THAT MAN ACTS AGAINST HIS OWN JUDGMENT

(b) It is objected that our scheme fails to account for all choices where the man acts against his own better judgment and prevalent feelings; or; in other words, that while the dictate of the understanding as to the truly preferable, is one way, the will acts the other way; e. g., the drunkard breaks his own anxiously made resolutions of temperance, and drinks. I reply, No; still the man has chosen according to what was the prevalent view of his judgment and feelings, as a whole, at the time. That drunkard does judge sobriety the preferable part in the end, and on the whole; but as to the question of this present glass of drink, (the only immediate object of volition,) his understanding is misinformed by strong propensity and the delusive hope of subsequent reform, combining the advantages of present indulgence with future impunity; so that its judgment is, that the preferable good will be this one glass, rather than present, immediate self-denial.

THAT REPENTANCE IMPLIES POWER OF CONTRARY CHOICE

(c) It is objected that our repentance for having chosen wrong, always implies the feeling that we might have chosen otherwise, had we pleased. I reply, Yes; but not unless that choice had been preceded at the time by a different view of the preferable. The thing for which the man blames himself is, that he had not those different feelings and views. (d.) It is objected that our theory could never account for a man's choosing between two alternative objects, equally accessible and desirable, inasmuch as the desire for either is equal, and the will has no self-deter- mining power. The answer is, that the equality of objects by no means implies the equality of subjective desires. For the mind is never in precisely the same state of feeling to any external object or objects, for two minutes together, but ever ebbing and flowing more or less. In this case, although the objects remain equal, the mind will easily make a difference, perhaps an imaginary one. And farther: the two objects being equal, the inertia of will towards choosing a given one of them, may be infinitesimally small; so that an infinitesimally small preponderance of subjective motive may suffice to overcome it. Remember, there is already a subjective motive in the general, to choose some one of them. A favorite instance supposed is that of a rich man, who has in his palm two or three golden guineas, telling a beggar that he may take any one. But they are exactly equal in value. Now, the beggar has a very positive motive to take some one of them, in his desire for the value to him of a guinea. The least imaginative impulse within his mind is enough to decide a supposed difference which is infinitesimal...

Motive, what? The Inducement not Motive

Most important light is thrown upon the subject, by the proper answer to the question, what is motive? The will not being, as we have seen, self-moved, what is it which precedes the volition, and is the true cause? I reply, by distinguishing between motive and inducement. The inducement is that external object, towards which the desire tends, in rising to choice. Thus, the gold seen by the thief is the inducement to his volition to steal. But the perception of the gold is not his motive to that volition. His motive is the cupidity of his own soul, projecting itself upon the gold. And this cupidity, (as in most instances of motive,) is a complex of certain conceptions of the intellect, and concupiscence of the heart; conceptions of various utilities of the gold, and concupiscence towards the pleasures which it could procure. The inducement is objective; the motive is subjective. The inducement is merely the occasion, the motive is the true cause of the resulting volition. The object which is the inducement projects no force into the thief's soul. On the contrary, it is the passive object of a force of soul projected upon it. The moral power is wholly from within out wards. The action is wholly that of the thief's soul, the inducement is only acted on. The proof of this all important view is in this case. The same purse of gold is seen, in the same circumstances of opportunity and privacy, by two men; the second is induced by it to steal; on the first, it had no such power. Why the difference? The difference must be subjective in the two men, because objectively, the two cases are identical. Your good sense leads you to explain the different results by the differing characters of the two men. You say: "It is because the first man was honest, the second covetous." That is to say, the causative efficiency which dictated the two volitions was, in each case, from within the two men's souls, not from the gold. Besides, the objects of sense are inert, dead, senseless, and devoid of will. It is simply foolish to conceive of them as emitting a moral activity. The thief is the only agent in the case.

SENSUALISTIC VIEW OF NECESSITY FALSE

This plain view sheds a flood of light on the doctrine of the will. A volition has always a cause, which is the (subjective) motive. This cause is efficient, otherwise the effect, volition, would not follow. But the motive is subjective; I. e., it is the agent judging and desiring, just as truly as the volition is the agent choosing. And this subjective desire, causative of the choice, is a function of the agent's activity, not of his passivity. The desire is as much of the agent's spontaneity (self-action) as is the choosing. Thus is corrected the monstrous view of those who deduced a doctrine of the necessity of the will from a sensualistic psychology. If volition is efficiently caused by desire, and if desire is but the passive reflex of objective perception, then, indeed, is man a mere machine. His seeming free-agency is wholly deceptive; and his choice is dictated from without. Then, indeed, the out-cry of the semi-Pelagian against such a necessity is just. But inducement is not motive; desire is an activity, and not a passivity of our souls. Our own subjective judgments and appetencies cause our volitions.

Inducement Receives Its Influence From The Subjective Disposition

On the other hand, it is equally plain, that the adaptation of any object to be an inducement to volition, depends on some subjective attribute of appetency in the agent. This state of appetency is *a priori* to the inducement, not created by it, but conferring on the object its whole fitness to be an inducement. In other words, when we seek to propagate a volition, by holding out an inducement as occasion, or means, we always presuppose in the agent whom we address, some active propensity. No one attempts to allure a hungry horse with bacon, or a hungry man with hay. Why! Common sense recognizes in each animal an a priori state of appetite, which has already determined to which of them the bacon shall be inducement, and to which the hay. The same thing is true of the spiritual desires, love of applause, of power, of justice, &c. Hence, it follows, that inducement has no power whatever to revolutionize the subjective states of appetency natural to an agent. The effect cannot determine its own cause.

From this point of view

may also be seen the justice of that philosophy of common sense, with which we set out; when we remarked that every one regarded a man's free acts as indices of an abiding or permanent character. This is only because the abiding appetencies of soul decide which objects shall be, and which shall not, be inducements to choice.

Freedom, What?

The student will perceive that I have not used the phrase, "freedom of the will." I exclude it, because persuaded that it is inaccurate, and that it has occasioned much confusion and error. Freedom is properly predicated of a person, not of a faculty. This was seen by Locke, who says, B. 2, ch. 21, sec. 10, "Liberty is not an idea belonging to volition, or preferring, but to the person having the power. This is so obviously true, as to need no argument. I have preferred therefore to use the phrase, at once popular and exact: "free agency," and "free agent" Turretin (Loc. x, Qu. I) sees this objection to the traditional term, *Liberum arbitrium,*" and hesitates about its use. But, after carefully defining it, he concedes to custom that it may be cautiously used, in the stipulated sense of the freedom of the Agent who wills. It would have been safer to change it.

I have also preferred to state and argue the old question as to the nature of free agency, in the common form it has borne in the history of theology, before I embarrassed the student with any of the attempted modifications of the doctrine. Locke, following the sensualistic definition, says that "liberty is the idea of a power in any agent to do or forbear any particular action, according to the determination or thought of the mind." But more profound analysts, as Reid and Cousin, saw that it consists in more than the sensualist would represent: mere privilege to execute outwardly what we have willed. My consciousness insists, that I am also a free Agent in having that volition. There, is the essential feature of choice; there, the rational preference first exhibits itself. The rational psychologists, consequently, assert the great, central truth, that the soul is self-determining. They see clearly that the soul, and not the objective inducement, is the true cause of its own acts of choice; and that hence man is justly responsible. But in order to sustain this central point, they vacillate towards the old Semi-Pelagian absurdity, that not only the man, but the separate faculty of will, is self-determined. They fail to grasp the real facts as to the nature and the power of subjective motive, the exercise of another set of faculties in the soul.

MOTIVE, WHAT?

Edwards saw more perspicaciously. Teaching that motive efficaciously determines the will, he defined motive, as all that which, together, moves the will to choice. It is always a complex of some view or judgment of the understanding,

and some movement of appetency or repulsion as to an object. These two elements must be, at least virtually and implicitly, in the precedaneous state of soul; or choice, volition, would not result. The intelligence has seen some object in the category of the true (or at least has thought it saw it thus), and the appetency has moved towards it as in the category of the desirable; else, no deliberate, affirmative volition had occurred. The mere presence and perception of the object is the occasion; the soul's own judgment and appetency form the cause of the act of choice.

Desire is not Passive

But what is appetency? If we conformed it with passion, with mere impression on natural sensibilities, we again fall into the fatal errors of the sensualist. Sir Wm. Hamilton has done yeoman's service to truth, by illustrating the difference (while he has claimed more than due credit for originating the distinction). He separates the passive powers of "sensibility," from the active powers of "conation." This is but the old (and correct) Calvinistic classification of the powers of the soul under "understanding," "affections," and will." Here, be it noted, the word "will" is taken, as in some places of our Confession, in a much wider sense than the specific faculty of choice. "Will" here includes all the active powers of the soul, and is synonymous with Sir Wm. Hamilton's "conative" powers. When we say, then, that man's soul is self-determining, we mean that, in the specific formation of choice, the soul choosing is determined by a complex of previous functions of the same soul seeing and desiring. In this sense the soul is free. But, as has been stated, no cause in the universe acts lawlessly. "Order is heaven's first law."

DISPOSITION
THE ALL-IMPORTANT FACT

And the regulative law of souls, when causing volitions, is found in their dispositions. This all important fact in free-agency, is what the scholastic divines called *Habitus* (not Consuetudo). It is the same notion popularly expressed by the word character. We know that man has such *habitus*, or disposition, which is more abiding than any access, or one series of acts of any one desire. For we deem that in a knave, for instance, evil disposition is present while he is eating, or laughing, or asleep, or while thinking anything else than his knavish plans. If we will reflect, we shall see that we intuitively ascribe disposition, of some sort, to every rational free agent: indeed we cannot think such an object without it. God, angel, demon, man, each is invariably conceived as having some abiding disposition, good or bad. It is in this that we find the regulative principle of the free-agency of all volition rises according to subjective motive. Subjective motive arises (freely) according to ruling subjective disposition. Disposition also is spontaneous—its very nature is to act freely. Here then, we have the two ultimate factors of free agency; Spontaneity, Disposition, Here we are at the end of all possible analysis. It is as vain to ask: "Why am I disposed thus?" as to seek a prior root of my spontaneity. The fact of my responsibility as a free agent does not turn on the answer to the question: it turns on this: that the disposition, which is actually my own will, regulates the rise freely of just the subjective motives I entertain. Let the student ponder my main argument (on pages 122 to 124) and he will see that in no other way is the free agency of ei-

McCosh's View of the Will

Dr. McCosh (Div. and Moral Gov. as cited in the syllabus,) wrests the true doctrine in some degree. He calls the will the "optative faculty," correctly distinguishing desire from sensibility, (which he terms emotion.) But he erroneously confounds appetency and volition together as the same functions of one power. That this is not correct, is evinced by one short question: May not the soul have two competing appetencies, and choose between them? We must hold fast, with the great body of philosophers, to the fact, that the power of decision, or choice, is unique, and not to be confounded even with subjective desires. It is the executive faculty. Dr. McCosh concedes that motive (as defined by Edwards) efficaciously decides the will; but he then asserts, with Coleridge, that the will determines motives. Conceding this, he has virtually surrendered his doctrine to the Arminian, and gotten around to a literal self-determination of the will. He seems to have been misled by an inaccurate glimpse of the truth I stated on p. 102, that the disposition determines a priori which sorts of objects shall be inducements to it. There is a two-fold confusion of this profound and important truth. Disposition is not the will; but a regulative principle of the appetencies, or "optative" functions, through them controlling the will. And, second, it is wholly another thing to say, that this disposition decides which objects shall be inducements, the occasions only of volitions; and to say with Dr. McCosh, that the will chooses among the soul's own subjective motives, the verae causae of the very acts of choice!

WATTS' VIEW

Dr. Isaac Watts, as is often stated, attempted to modify the doctrine of the will, by supposing that we had inverted the order of cause and effect. He deemed that we do not choose an object because we have desired it; but that we desire it because we have chosen it. In other words, he thought desire the result, and not the forerunner of choice. This scheme obviously leaves the question unanswered: How do volitions arise? And by seeming to leave them without cause, he favors the erroneous scheme of the Arminian. It is enough to say, that no man's consciousness, properly examined, will bear out this position. Do we not often have desires where, in consequence of other causes in the mind, we form no volition at all? This question will be seen decisive.

BLEDSOE'S VIEW

Dr. Albert Taylor Bledsoe, in his Reply to Edwards, Theodicy, and other essays, attempts to modify the Arminian theory, without surrendering it. He is too perspicacious to say, with the crowd of semi-Pelagians, that volitions are uncaused results in the mental world; he knows too well the universality of the great, necessary intuition, ex *nihilo nihil.* But denying that motives, even subjective, are cause of acts of choice, he says the mind is the immediate cause of them. He seems here to approach very near the orthodox view. Even Dr. Alexander could say, while denying the self-determination of the will, that he was ready to admit the self-determination of the mind. But this concession of Dr. Bledsoe does not bring him to the correct ground. It leaves the question unexplained, in what way the mind is determined from within to choice. It refuses to accept the efficient influence of subjective motive. It still asserts that any volition may be contingent as to its use, thus embodying the essential features of Arminianism. And above all: it fails to see or admit the most fundamental fact of all; that original disposition which regulates each being's desires and volitions. The applications which this author makes of his modified doctrine betray still its essential Arminianism.

In conclusion, it is only necessary at this place to say in one word, that the disposition which is found in every natural man, as to God and godliness, is depravity. Hence his will, according to the theory expounded above, is, in the Scriptural sense, in bondage to sin, while he remains properly a free and responsible agent.

NOTES

The antiquity of this cavil, and its proper refutation, may be seen in the *Cur Deus Homo* of Anselm, pt. 2, chap. 10, where the topic is the impeccability of Christ.

BOSO.—"I say, then, if He *cannot sin,* because, as you say, He cannot wish to, He obeys from necessity; whence, He is not righteous from the freedom of His will. Then, what favour will be due Him for His righteousness? For we are wont to say, that God, therefore, made angels and men such that they could sin; since, inasmuch as they could forsake righteousness, and could keep righteousness out of the freedom of their will, they would deserve approbation and favour, which would not be due to them were they righteous from necessity."

ANSELM.—"Are the (elect) angels who now cannot sin, to be approved or not?"

BOSO.—"Of course they are, because this gift (that they cannot sin) they earned in this way, viz.: by not choosing to sin when they could."

ANSELM.—"Well, what do you say about God, who is not able to sin, and yet did not earn that state by not choosing to sin while He had the power to do it: isn't He to be praised for His righteousness?"

BOSO.—"I wish you would answer for me there; for, if I say He is not to be praised for it, I know I am lying; but if I say He is, I am afraid I shall spoil that argument of mine about the angels."

Anselm proceeds, accepting this virtual confession of defeat, to explain: That the approvableness of the angels' conduct depends, not on the question, "*How they came by* the dispositions which prompt them to obey;" but on the question, *whether they have such dispositions, and act them out of their own accord:* That God, in creating them with free-agency, intelligence and holy dispositions, conferred His own image upon them; and that their spontaneity, though conferred, is as real, and as really moral, as God's spontaneity, which was not conferred, but eternal and necessary. And that, if there were any force in Boso's cavil, that a morally necessitated righteousness would not be free and approvable in the creature, it would be far stronger against God, whose holiness is the most strictly necessitated of all, being absolutely eternal.

ROBERT LEWIS DABNEY

Free Agency and the Will

ROBERT LEWIS DABNEY

Free Agency and the Will

ROBERT LEWIS DABNEY

www.ingramcontent.com/pod-product-compliance
Lightning Source LLC
Chambersburg PA
CBHW071756080526
44588CB00013B/2265